MIND
EXPANSION

DANIEL MCMEANS

"Mind Expansion," by Daniel McMeans ISBN 978-1-63868-202-8.

Published 2025 by Virtualbookworm.com Publishing, P.O. Box 9949, College Station, TX 77842, US. Copyright ©2025, Daniel McMeans.

Table of Contents

CONTENT INFLUENCES YOUR BEINGNESS

Content has the power to transform your being. Your mindset and consciousness gradually shift as you immerse yourself in positive and spiritual material. Knowledge impacts the brain by creating new neural connections and strengthening existing ones through neuroplasticity. Over time, this content becomes integrated with your life in alignment with God's will. Prayer plays a significant role in this process, as it sets the intention for your transformation. When I embarked on this journey of self-growth, I sought guidance through a combination of New Age spiritual teachings and ancient religious texts. This holistic approach allowed me to assimilate a wide range of insights, offering a well-rounded path to growth.

From my experience, I can attest that prayer and reading God-inspired literature bring about profound change. It strengthens your spirit, builds discipline, sharpens your focus, provides guidance, and propels you forward with vitality. But it is essential to remember that this transformation requires commitment from you. This energy moves you forward because it draws from an infinite source—God's boundless power. When we tap into this divine source, we align ourselves with His abundance, which becomes the foundation of our growth. This core connection enables us to progress and become better versions of ourselves.

Each person is unique, and as you walk this path of growth, you aren't losing that individuality. Rather, God knows how to integrate your uniqueness with the wisdom and guidance you are receiving. Praying and asking God to help you incorporate your personal traits into this new journey is crucial because everything begins with intention. The most important thing is to live a purposeful life, one that reflects the belief that nothing is impossible for you when you align yourself with divine will, which reflects your inherent nature.

DIVINITY IN MATH

Let's entertain the idea that God, in His infinite wisdom, used something akin to an algebraic formula to initiate and expand the universe through what we now understand as the Big Bang. Mathematics, so often seen as a human tool, might very well be a divine language, woven into the very fabric of creation.

Today, math touches nearly every aspect of our lives—whether it's used in cooking, budgeting, managing time, designing buildings, advancing medical research, or creating digital technology. It's the foundation for measuring, analyzing, and identifying the patterns that shape our understanding of the world. The ability to make informed decisions, drawn from observation and analysis, is rooted in the logic and precision of mathematics.

This idea isn't new. During the Renaissance, a period of incredible human advancement in the 16th century, mathematics, art, and science merged in remarkable ways. This era gave rise to some of the most brilliant minds in history. Leonardo da Vinci, deeply spiritual and visionary, integrated his love of God with a profound understanding of geometry and proportion, using mathematics as a foundation for his groundbreaking inventions and artwork.

Michelangelo, whose work on the Sistine Chapel still leaves people in awe, also operated with divine inspiration. He embraced the Golden Ratio, a mathematical principle found throughout nature, to guide the harmony and balance in his art, reflecting the beauty of God's creation.

Galileo, often called the father of modern science, relied heavily on math to describe the natural world. He pioneered the use of measurement and algebraic analysis, laying the groundwork for scientific inquiry as we know it today.

Fast forward to the 20th century: Edwin Hubble, after whom the Hubble Space Telescope is named, used mathematics to show the expansion of the universe, lending crucial support to the Big Bang Theory and reshaping our understanding of the cosmos.

Think about it... after the Big Bang, the Earth ended up just the proper distance from the Sun, allowing life to flourish. We benefit from the sun's vitamin D; plants perform photosynthesis, sustaining ecosystems. Can all of this truly be random? The precision and harmony are staggering. The majesty of God defies human comprehension. He exists beyond the limits of time, space, and logic, yet His fingerprints are all over creation—from the spirals of galaxies to the symmetry in a leaf.

Let us move forward with love and intention, embracing the mystery and presence of God all around us. In math, nature, art, and science, we are reminded: the Divine is everywhere, waiting for us to notice.

DREAMS

Dreams tap into the subconscious mind, potentially providing insights into one's spiritual self. These spiritual truths, or messages from a higher power, connect us to a spiritual dimension. Dreams often contain symbolic imagery that can be interpreted as messages from the spirit realm. Paul McCartney openly discussed that he was inspired by his dreams when he wrote the lyrics to "Let it Be". James Cameron, the director, explained how he was influenced by his dreams to produce and direct "Avatar". Even Albert Einstein was influenced by dreams, ultimately leading to "The Theory of Relativity."

The Prophet Daniel received messages of divine communication, allowing him to predict future events, particularly regarding the rise and fall of kingdoms. This solidified his role as a mighty prophet and interpreter of God's will. He was often called upon to interpret the dreams of key rulers, like King Nebuchadnezzar, further establishing his position in the court. During this time, Daniel was punished for his talents and even thrown into a den of lions for the night; however, he was ultimately saved by the grace of God.

Over the years, dreams have influenced the landscape in many ways. Dreams inspired the arts during the Renaissance Era in the 15th century. They have also guided us in the study of physics and science. Dreams of inspiration, delivered by our spiritual beliefs, can give us hope for a better tomorrow.

Evoking Music

Throughout human history, music has carried profound spiritual meaning. Across centuries and cultures, it has served as a sacred bridge between humanity and the divine. From ancient chants to modern hymns, music has always been integral to worship—lifting hearts, deepening faith, and awakening a sense of connection to something greater than ourselves. Music has played a central role in spiritual life, whether in Christianity, Buddhism, Hinduism, or Islam.

When paired with faith, music enhances our understanding of God's grace, revealing it as beautiful, abundant, and ever-flowing, touching every corner of the universe. God's sovereignty is vast and layered, and His love has no boundaries. As we walk with Him, we begin to understand that His presence is not confined to temples, churches, or holy texts. He is with us at every moment—when we're watching TV, sitting alone in thought, or turning the pages of a book. He is not a distant God who appears only during rituals; He is always near, always present.

We must expand our understanding of His abundance to truly connect with this divine presence. His power knows no limits, and music is one of the most powerful tools through which we experience His essence. Across genres and

7

generations, music glorifies God in unique ways, carrying His message in melodies, rhythms, and lyrics that resonate deep within the soul.

Music is energy, and energy is one of the many forms through which God expresses Himself. The divine emits a vast spectrum of energetic vibrations, each reflecting a different facet of His being. This is a crucial perspective to embrace: energy is not just a scientific concept; it is spiritual. Joy, grief, peace, confusion…they are all forms of energy. And when we begin to see life through this lens, we empower ourselves to navigate emotional and spiritual shifts with greater ease and awareness.

By recognizing this energetic flow, we can consciously move from one state of being to another, with prayer as our anchor. When we pray, we're not just speaking—we're tuning ourselves to God's frequency, aligning our energy with His, and allowing His grace to carry us from sorrow to peace, from confusion to clarity.

In this light, music becomes more than art. It becomes a vessel of divine energy, a healing force, and a language of the soul. Through it, we draw closer to God's heart.

FROM THE CORE OF OUR BEING

At the very core of who we are lies a powerful truth: the energy we choose to align with shapes the direction of our lives. Every decision, every emotion, and every intention sends energy into motion. Some energies are more impactful, sustainable, and aligned with our higher purpose than others.

It's easy to notice that negative energy often delivers fast results. But those results come at a cost. They're built on fear, control, and scarcity—tactics that may yield immediate outcomes but ultimately weaken and erode over time. In contrast, positive energy—like inspiration, compassion, and hope—builds slowly but echoes far wider. It creates a ripple effect on the human experience that multiplies exponentially. Why is this?

Positive energy originates from Divine Truth. When something flows from the Divine, it carries infinite potential. That's the energy worth investing in. The difference comes down to intention. When we set an intention rooted in love, faith, and purpose, we unlock a current of unseen forces working in our favor—opening doors, shifting perspectives, and allowing the impossible to become real.

Over the course of my life, I've come to believe that anything is possible when you truly commit to that mindset. Belief, paired with repetition, creates results. The brain responds to consistency—each time we repeat a thought or action, we're strengthening neural connections, keeping the mind sharp and aligned with growth.

And that brings us to the idea of mind expansion. What is mind expansion, really? It's the process of narrowing the gap between faith and fear. The more you choose faith, through worship, prayer, and spiritual focus, the less power fear holds over your life. As fear diminishes, so do the emotional attachments that weigh us down: bitterness, jealousy, addiction, judgment, and low self-worth.

When you begin to release these burdens, you start to live more boldly, more freely, and with a deeper sense of love and purpose. Life becomes more than survival; it becomes an expression of divine alignment.

So, let's choose to live with intentional love. Let's move forward with purpose and align with the kind of energy that not only lifts us but uplifts the world around us. Because when you connect to the infinite source of Divine Truth, your path forward is limitless.

GOD'S GRACE

When you begin walking the path of enlightenment, it's natural to feel a pull toward prayer—a moment to ask God for guidance and meaningful change. Depending on your intentions, your heart's desires, and your karmic journey, God responds in His own time and way, helping align your mind with your higher self and softening the grip of ego.

As you grow spiritually, you may start to notice God's presence more deeply in your life, which can lead you to reflect inwardly. In that stillness, you may become more aware of ego-based traits such as bitterness, jealousy, the need to control, or a tendency to find fault. Recognizing these qualities is the first step toward transformation.

I encourage you to bring these realizations into your prayer life. Ask God for help in dissolving the ego's grip. These patterns often carry deep roots and their own form of consciousness, so letting go may not happen overnight. But with consistent faith and prayer—even just a few times a week—you can begin to release what no longer serves your soul.

Surrendering the ego isn't about defeat; it's about letting go of self-centered motives and opening yourself to God's Grace—His unconditional love, favor, and guidance.

Through prayer, we become more aligned with divine will and more attuned to our true intentions and purpose.

Each day is a new opportunity to rise with purpose and approach life with passion. With a clear vision for the future, we can build momentum toward meaningful goals while also taking time to reflect on the past. Our mistakes aren't failures; they are lessons, stepping stones that help us grow into deeper awareness and fulfillment.

In striving for higher consciousness, reflection, intention, and grace become the pillars of a truly awakened life.

SPIRITUAL BELIEFS IN ASTROLOGY

In many spiritual circles today, astrology is viewed not just as a tool for prediction, but as a meaningful framework for understanding ourselves and our place in the cosmos. The idea is that celestial bodies—the sun, moon, and planets—emit subtle energies that influence our lives in ways both personal and profound. By studying their positions at the time of our birth, we can uncover insights into our personalities, life paths, and even deeper spiritual lessons.

This belief system has deep roots in traditions like Hinduism, where astrology (or Jyotish) is used to align human life with cosmic rhythms. Birth charts are interpreted to help individuals navigate key life decisions, karmic patterns, and their journey toward self-realization. Similarly, many New Age approaches embrace astrology as a way to track spiritual growth, offering a lens through which to interpret life's patterns and lessons.

At the core of these beliefs is a sense of **cosmic interconnectedness**, the idea that everything in the universe is interwoven, and that the movement of the planets reflects a larger, intelligent design. Some also see astrology as a form of divine guidance, where planetary alignments serve as symbolic messages or spiritual signposts.

Beyond the metaphysical, astrology serves a practical role in encouraging self-awareness and personal growth. Many use it to better understand their behavioral tendencies, relational dynamics, and areas for development, treating it as a reflective tool rather than a rigid script.

Today, astrology remains an integral part of various spiritual paths, especially within New Age spirituality, where it's often combined with practices like meditation, energy healing, and mindfulness to support a more conscious and aligned way of living.

CONNECTIVITY

To truly solve a problem and get the greatest return, you need to approach it from the inside out. Surface-level fixes won't do much if the core system is broken—it's like trying to polish an engine that isn't running. Without addressing the root causes, any solution will be incomplete and yield minimal results.

Real progress begins when you confront foundational issues head-on. That's what brings clarity, smoother collaboration, and greater effectiveness. When everything is aligned at the core, moving forward and building momentum toward your goals becomes much easier.

Of course, not every job or role allows for this kind of creative problem-solving or meaningful contribution. But even if your work isn't the most fulfilling, your hobbies and side pursuits can still be a rich outlet for creativity. When you merge your imagination with inner purpose, it can deeply nourish your sense of self.

Before taking any action, take the time to reflect, understand the challenges, and build a plan. If your beliefs are grounded in something greater—like faith or purpose—they can help anchor you and guide your choices with love, trust, and authenticity.

The goal is to channel your energy into something meaningful. A life of purpose is one shaped by your values and passions, where you grow, contribute, and find fulfillment. That's what creates lasting impact—not just for yourself but for the world around you.

As Lewis Grizzard once said, "If you're not the lead dog, the view never changes." So take the lead—starting from within.

Overcoming Depression

Depression often stems from prolonged exposure to stress, unresolved trauma, self-doubt, or deeply ingrained fear. These emotional burdens don't just fade on their own… they require attention and care, whether through professional support from a therapist or doctor, or through complementary healing practices like energy work.

One way to begin the process of healing is by becoming more conscious of what you allow into your mental and emotional space. What you consume—mentally, emotionally, and spiritually—shapes your inner world. The ancient wisdom "As above, so below; as within, so without" reminds us that we are reflections of the larger universe, and with belief in ourselves and connection to our higher self, even the greatest challenges can be transformed.

Exploring the potential of your own mind is essential. The more you stretch your thinking and open yourself to new levels of growth and achievement, the more you align with your deeper purpose. Immersing yourself in positive, empowering ideas helps you reframe fear and invites expansion, clarity, and resilience.

When fear no longer dominates your thoughts, creativity and vision can flourish. You start imagining possibilities that weren't visible before—ideas that not only uplift you but can also inspire and heal those around you. In this way, healing becomes both a personal and collective act.

This is, in many ways, the rhythm of the universe. When we encounter blocks in life, the answer isn't always to force our way through them. Instead, it's about reconnecting with the belief that we hold immense potential within. Through faith—in ourselves and in something greater—we tap into the energy needed to move forward with purpose and strength.

As Buddha once said, "Our life is shaped by our *mind;* we become what we think." And so, with conscious thought and belief, healing becomes not just possible, it becomes inevitable.

LIFE EXPANDS FROM THE MIND

Let's talk about **faith**, the unwavering foundation that supports you through life's highs and lows. It's crucial to remain anchored in your beliefs, especially when faced with challenges. When you stand firm in your faith, you can weather any storm, no matter how fierce. Your faith becomes the rock you lean on, and nothing can shake you from that position of strength.

Faith has a remarkable ability to overcome fear and negative emotions—anger, envy, greed, judgment, and jealousy. These shadows can cloud our minds and hearts, but faith brings light, clarity, and peace. It radiates outward, impacting not just your own life but the world around you. Like a spark that ignites a chain reaction, positive energy moves through humanity, shifting the collective consciousness and spreading hope across the globe.

Some might say life isn't fair, but there's truth in the belief that with hard work, courage, and boldness, you can turn the odds in your favor. As John Milton wisely put it, "Luck is the residue of design." Life, much like a rubber band, will stretch and contract. But if you invest in your goals and make sacrifices, you'll find that the peaks outnumber the valleys. The energy of the universe responds to your efforts and your heart's intent, manifesting the right opportunities at the right time.

At the core of this cosmic balance is Love—the infinite and all-encompassing force that connects everything. Love is the universal law that binds us all. It is the driving force behind creation, the energy that brings harmony, and the power that heals. As Dr. Wayne Dyer, a modern-day mystic, once said, *"Hate converts to love when the energy of love is in its presence."* Love from God is the highest form of healing energy, transcending all limitations and offering a power that only the Divine can emit. This is the force that sustains us and elevates humanity.

LIFE LESSONS ON EARTH

According to spiritual teachings, we are always exposed to life lessons on earth as we evolve towards a higher consciousness. These include lessons about love, compassion, forgiveness and responsibility. We also experience life lessons in connection with nature, overcoming ego, embracing change, and facing challenges with resilience. Our ultimate goal is finding inner peace through prayer and unity with all living things.

Relationships

Navigating complex relationships with others to learn how to communicate, show empathy, establish boundaries, and demonstrate unconditional love.

Acceptance

Embracing life's challenges, imperfections, and diversity.

Forgiveness

Letting go of resentments and negative feelings towards oneself and others. Learning to love yourself so you can learn to love others.

Connection to Nature

Recognizing the interconnectedness of all living things and respecting the environment.

The key is investing your energy in living a purposeful life, guided by your values and passions. This allows you to contribute to the world in a meaningful way. It involves establishing a direction for your life to continue growing and learning. When you determine your life's purpose, you are in tune with yourself and understand the interaction between your thoughts and experiences. These are often interpreted as signs from a higher power, signifying a deep connection between your inner self and the external world. As we move through life, we are always faced with opportunities to change and evolve if we stay alert to the subtle messages sent by our higher power.

LOVE

Love is often seen as a complex and multifaceted emotion encompassing many positive mental and emotional experiences. It is about connection—a deep bond between people marked by affection, respect, and shared understanding. Love can stem from kinship, friendship, admiration, or simple tenderness.

But beyond individual relationships, love is the universal force that binds humanity. We need to invest more in this because it holds the potential to create lasting change in the world. The energy of love is infinite—it originates from a higher source, and that source is God. Love is abundant and boundless in its purest form, yet many of us fail to tap into this limitless resource to its fullest potential.

The intangible forces of love, faith, and the belief in the impossible hold incredible power. These concepts can overcome even the most daunting obstacles. But it all starts with intention: a commitment to channeling energy into what we believe in. When we focus on the shared values that unite us as people, regardless of our differences, we start to see that we all strive for the same fundamental truths and aspirations.

One of the most important lessons we can learn is the importance of tolerance. Everyone has their own perspective and journey, but we are all God's children, each on our own path toward greater awareness and enlightenment. Our differences don't divide us, they offer the opportunity to learn and grow together.

Ultimately, love is the greatest force of grace, transcending human understanding. It reaches beyond our limited capacities because it is rooted in the Divine. As we move forward, let's commit to investing more love and energy into our beliefs, creating a ripple effect that fosters understanding and unity.

MANIFESTATION – CAN OPTIMISM CHANGE REALITY?

A 2007 study led by neuroscientist Elisabeth Phelps uncovered fascinating insights into how our brains function when we focus on positive thoughts. Specifically, directing our intentions toward the frontal cortex—a region constantly interacting with deeper brain areas—seems to play a pivotal role in shaping our mental and emotional landscapes.

Expanding the mind is essential for unlocking its limitless potential. Our thoughts can transcend the ordinary and reach the farthest corners of our imagination. If we believe in the mind's infinite capacity, we open ourselves to a life of boundless awareness. In essence, when we embrace our full potential, we can achieve the impossible, like moving mountains.

Our expectations shape our reality, acting as self-fulfilling prophecies. How we perceive our abilities and future outcomes directly influences our actions, guiding what unfolds ahead.

Materialization—turning thoughts into reality—occurs when our brain, particularly the deep regions, receives positive intentions from the cortex and transmits this energy outward into the universe. This cosmic exchange understands our needs and desires, setting the steps to manifest them in motion.

Interestingly, recent studies show striking similarities between the human brain and the vast network of galaxies in the cosmos. The same atoms and molecules that make up our brains are present throughout the universe, highlighting a profound interconnectedness. When we project positive thoughts into the world, the universe responds, aligning its forces to bring those thoughts into physical existence. (Contributing *material from Times Magazine*)

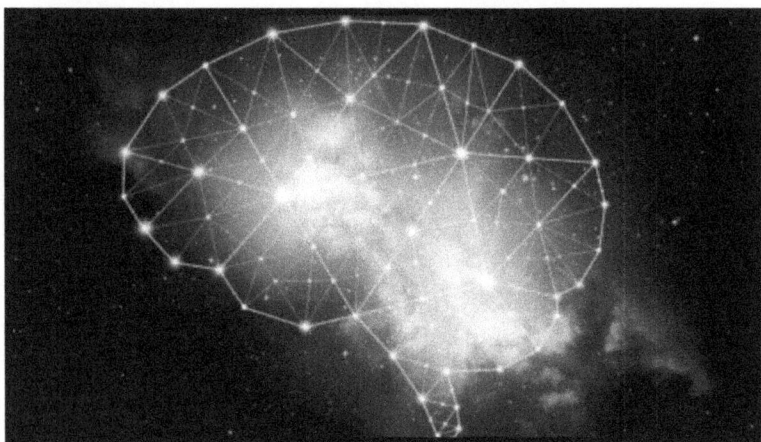

MARRIAGE

Based on available evidence from early human societies, marriage likely originated around 23,000 years ago. However, these early unions were far different from the concept of marriage we know today. Back then, marriage was less about romantic love and more about creating strategic alliances between families. Parents typically arranged these marriages to strengthen social and economic standing rather than out of personal affection.

As time passes and people grow older, both individuals in a marriage inevitably change. Our values shift, and we evolve in ways we might not have anticipated when we first entered the relationship. The key to a lasting partnership is embracing each other's growth, supporting each other's evolving ideas, passions, and hobbies. This willingness to grow together is fundamental. A couple that learns to adapt and build a strong foundation through the years is likelier to enter their later years with a sense of unity and mutual respect. Early marriage vows were essentially the blueprint for this, providing a structure for couples to navigate the complexities of life together.

However, despite the ideal, the reality is that 50% of marriages end in divorce, often within the first seven years.

Divorce is an emotionally charged experience, usually bringing out the worst in people. Feelings of bitterness and resentment can arise, which, if left unresolved, may lead to psychological stress, strained relationships, and even physical health issues.

To move through a divorce with the least emotional damage, it's crucial to maintain as much peace and cooperation as possible, especially when children are involved. The focus should shift from past grievances to the possibility of a happier future, where both individuals can heal and move forward, separately but peacefully.

Mind Expansion for Treatment of Depression

In today's world, we often find ourselves consumed by the material. That's why it's crucial to be mindful of the content we consume, especially regarding what we read and expose ourselves to. The information we take in directly impacts our brain, influencing its neural pathways. Focusing on positive, uplifting content, we help our brain reorganize and strengthen its synaptic connections, generating electrical signals that activate thousands of neurons in the prefrontal cortex.

This process isn't just about calming the mind; it's about setting the stage for a fresh start—a new beginning that can positively affect years of your life.

We must understand the vast potential of our minds. It's essential to believe that we have the power to change our reality and move mountains by expanding our capabilities. When we allow ourselves to unlock this potential, we can reach new heights, achieve excellence, and fulfill our life's purpose.

And that's what it's all about...discovering and living your life's purpose.

Once we tap into this potential, the world opens up to us. Our imagination becomes limitless, and from this creative freedom, new ideas flow—ideas that emerge only when we're free from fear. When faced with negativity, the key is to maintain the right mindset. How we approach challenges determines how we overcome them.

If you start each day with the energy and brightness of the sun, with the intention of putting one foot in front of the other and dedicating yourself to your goals, you honor your purpose. By focusing on what lies ahead, not dwelling on the past, you'll be equipped to face negativity with grace and resilience. As Jesus said, "The one who seeks should not cease seeking until he finds."

MISTAKES FUEL SUCCESS

Trial and error is a fundamental principle of growth. When practiced with intention and consistent reflection, it leads to tangible results. This process has a natural synergy, especially when you take the time to assess your actions and measure your progress. With commitment, this approach becomes a powerful tool for success.

During my time as a territory sales manager, I frequently made sales presentations to various accounts. Not every presentation was a success, and when they weren't, I'd return home and reflect on the objections I faced. I'd think about how to find common ground and create win-win outcomes. It wasn't always easy—it required deep thought and problem-solving—but I realized that rejection and mistakes were crucial learning opportunities. They helped me sharpen my skills and become more effective at what I did.

The more consistently you invest in learning from your failures and mistakes, the more successful you'll become. There's an inherent system at play—an unseen structure designed for you that operates when you stay committed and put in the work.

As Deepak Chopra wisely said, "Whatever you project, will come back to you." It's as simple as that. The more effort, focus, and energy you pour into your goals, the more the universe will return to you in the form of manifestations and opportunities.

Another key to propelling yourself forward is cultivating a positive mindset. When you think positively, your prefrontal cortex is activated, which in turn sends signals to deeper areas of your brain. These signals transmit positive energy to the universe, which responds by helping to manifest your efforts and hard work into reality.

This is a well-designed system, but it's up to you to tap into it, reach for it, and take ownership of it.

MOTHER EARTH

One of the greatest gifts Mother Earth provides is the essential foundation for life itself—clean air, water, food, and shelter. These resources are vital to our survival and overall well-being, forming the cornerstone of human existence.

Mother Earth serves as the life-sustaining system for all living beings. The air we breathe, coupled with the intricate design of our lungs, is part of a carefully balanced system that sustains life. This system, designed by a higher intelligence, supports not only humanity but also a vast diversity of plant and animal species, all of which play a crucial role in maintaining a healthy and balanced ecosystem. Countless medicines and healing treatments are derived from natural sources found right here on Earth.

Spending time in nature has been proven to enhance mental health by lowering stress levels and encouraging relaxation. Simple experiences like listening to the rhythmic sound of ocean waves or feeling the soothing presence of nature can significantly reduce stress. The ocean, for example, is full of healing minerals like magnesium, calcium, and potassium, which have a calming effect on the mind and body. Swimming in the sea can provide real mental health benefits.

Mother Earth also provides energy resources, like oil, through a natural process. Over millions of years, ancient marine organisms such as algae and zooplankton undergo decomposition under heat and pressure, turning into the hydrocarbon mixture we use as oil. This process, driven by natural forces, transforms the remains of life into an essential energy source.

When you consider the design of our planet, it's clear that Mother Earth functions according to a divine plan. The Earth and the Sun are perfectly positioned in space, allowing photosynthesis to occur, which helps plants grow and provides us with the vitamin D we need from sunlight. This intricate balance ensures our vegetables are nutrient-rich and sustain us. It's a powerful reminder of the intelligence and care behind the systems that nurture us.

It's evident that divine intelligence is at work in the world— a force that sustains us and supports all life, providing for our needs in ways that often go unnoticed.

NATURE SPIRITS

Nature spirits exist in many forms, each contributing to our understanding of the universe and the divine forces that shape it. These spirits, whether in the form of celestial bodies, flowing streams, or even trees, are part of a harmonious system that responds to our requests for guidance and blessings. Some believe that every element of nature carries divine energy, and these spirits are manifestations of nature's forces. By embracing this connection, we open ourselves to a deeper relationship with the natural world and its spiritual dimensions.

When I seek to connect with the nature spirits, I often visit a peaceful stream tucked away in Pennypack Park. It's a place where I can feel the subtle presence of these energies. You can connect with nature's spirits anywhere—whether you're in a forest, walking through a park, or even spending time in your own backyard.

I often recite the following prayer to facilitate this connection:

"Supreme Holy God, not my will, but Your Divine will, for the highest good and outcome. Please allow me to connect with the spirits of nature, guiding me toward healing and well-being. May Your loving energy cleanse me of all impurities and bring me closer to You, and may I honor You in all Your glory and blessings."

Amen

Regular prayer is an essential practice for maintaining emotional and spiritual well-being. It creates a space for connection with a Higher Power, bringing peace, gratitude, and hope into your life. Through prayer, we also find moments of reflection that help reduce stress and shift our mindset toward positivity.

NEW AGE SPIRITUALITY

New Age Spirituality highlights the importance of self-exploration, a crucial step in personal growth and fulfillment. By diving deep into this process, we better understand who we are, how we relate to others, and our place in the greater universe.

Through my journey with New Age Spirituality, I discovered countless opportunities for self-improvement. As I continued down this path, a new world appeared. I immersed myself in spiritual texts, blending insights from modern New Age teachings with wisdom from ancient religious traditions. This transformation not only reshaped my perspective on life, but it also led to unexpected breakthroughs. Along the way, I earned certifications focused on energy's impact on well-being and studied how neural pathways affect our physical and mental health. These experiences solidified my belief that we can't thrive without nurturing both mind and body.

As you embark on this journey, a new sense of clarity and self-confidence will naturally emerge. Embrace this newfound awareness with love, an entrepreneurial mindset, and a sense of responsibility. This level of consciousness brings a sense of freedom, but with freedom comes accountability. True abundance unfolds when you align your spirit with intentional actions and live in harmony with your core values.

There are a few guiding principles to carry with you as you move forward. These principles hold tremendous power but require daily attention and action to truly come to life. Trust that the thoughts and intentions you send into the universe can manifest in meaningful ways. Your belief in their potential is the essential first step to bringing them into reality.

POSITIVE FRAME OF MIND

Discipline in daily life and maintaining a positive mindset are key to personal well-being. Every thought we have triggers a chemical response in our brain. We often feel happier and more optimistic when we actively cultivate positive thoughts. This is due to the release of endorphins, reduced cortisol levels, and increased serotonin production. Normal serotonin levels help stabilize our emotions, reducing anxiety and promoting a sense of calm and happiness.

Let's focus on the prefrontal cortex of the brain. When positive thoughts arise, we see fundamental changes in the frontal lobe, where neurons are activated and new pathways are formed. This brain growth occurs as positive thought patterns are reinforced.

The brain plays a pivotal role in unlocking the power of our minds. When we harness this power, there are virtually no limits to what we can achieve in the material world. The potential of the material world is vast compared to the power of our spirit and belief. When you believe in yourself, nothing is impossible.

To truly maximize our lives, we must move beyond fear. Fear holds us back and limits our growth. Overcoming it is essential for reaching our full potential. Reading positive content can be powerful in challenging fear and expanding our minds. As we do this, we open ourselves up to limitless imagination, leading to innovative ideas born from living free of fear.

THIS IS HOW GOD'S UNIVERSE WORKS

As we embrace the path of positive thinking, it's crucial to remember not to judge others. We often ask, "What is normal?" Dr. David Gupta suggests that perhaps the person we're judging feels perfectly normal because they live according to their own definition of normality. He explains that everyone sets their own standards, and individuals should be free to live in their own positive reality, without being held back or oppressed. When imagination aligns with our inner spark, it unleashes a powerful wave of positive energy.

WHAT IS NORMAL?

Who defines "normal"? Throughout history, some of the most influential figures have challenged society's perceptions of normality, like Lord Jesus, Galileo, and Albert Einstein. Each of these individuals defied the conventional views of their time.

Lord Jesus sparked a revolution by teaching the transformative power of forgiveness and its profound impact on life. His teachings laid the foundation for Christianity, challenging societal norms with messages of love, compassion, and spiritual renewal.

Galileo, on the other hand, risked everything by declaring that the Earth revolved around the sun... an idea that went against the church's teachings. He was summoned to trial and branded a heretic for his belief, yet his discoveries forever altered our understanding of the cosmos.

Albert Einstein revolutionized how we understand the universe with his Theory of Relativity. His groundbreaking work showed that gravity, as we perceive it, is a result of the curvature of space and time, a radical departure from prior scientific thought.

In the end, the timeless truth remains: "Be yourself." Embrace your unique qualities, let your authentic self shine through, and allow your individuality to inspire and connect with others.

POSITIVE THOUGHT ENTITIES

When we interact with others, we must be mindful of our thoughts. Our brains are electromagnetic, meaning that our thoughts are transmitted to those around us. These thoughts can have a powerful influence on the people in our environment.

Experts like Master Choa Kok Sui and Dr. Bradley Nelson explain that thoughts and emotions create energetic forms known as "thought forms" or "emotional thought entities." These are essentially living, dynamic energy patterns that can impact others' behavior and emotions.

Our brains produce these thought entities through the complex interactions between billions of neurons that fire electrical impulses and release neurotransmitters. This process creates neural pathways that encode sensory data, memories, and experiences, effectively shaping how we think and feel and ultimately affecting those around us.

Ancient wisdom suggests that thought forms are made of energy and consist of both emotional and mental components. This is why focusing on sending positive and loving thoughts toward others is crucial. Even research shows that plants grow better when spoken to with care. Imagine the transformative effect of speaking loving, nurturing words to the people around us, helping them grow and thrive in ways we might not even realize.

Our conduct is at the heart of all this. We need to be more conscious of our thoughts because they play a key role in creating a more peaceful and harmonious world.

QUANTUM HEALING AND US

Quantum healing is a holistic practice that blends principles from quantum physics, psychology, and spirituality. It operates on the belief that the human body is biological and energetic… governed by quantum principles. In this framework, illness is seen as a disruption or imbalance within the body's energetic field.

The Energy Body

Our physical form comprises subatomic particles that emit and interact within an energetic field, often referred to as the aura. This field surrounds and permeates the body, acting as an interface between physical health and energetic balance.

Healing Through Consciousness

One of the foundational ideas in quantum healing is that we can access higher states of consciousness to initiate healing from within. By aligning our thoughts, emotions, and intentions, we can balance our quantum energy field by promoting emotional clarity and physical well-being.

Energy Healing Modalities

Techniques such as Pranic Healing, Reiki, and Shamanic practices are commonly used to work with the body's subtle energies. These practices aim to harmonize and recharge the energy system, supporting the healing of both emotional and physical ailments.

What Is Pranic Healing?

Pranic Healing works by tapping into the body's life force—or prana—to accelerate natural healing. Based on the principle that the body is inherently self-repairing, this technique cleanses and energizes the energy centers (chakras) to restore vitality and function.

What Is Reiki?

Reiki, though modernized in the 20th century by Dr. Mikao Usui, traces its origins back to ancient spiritual traditions. In 1922, Dr. Usui reportedly discovered the healing symbols of Reiki during a meditative retreat on Mount Kurama in Japan. Reiki uses universal energy to promote harmony across the mind, body, and spirit.

Mind Expansion and Inner Growth

Mind expansion is the practice of transcending fear and ego to access deeper wisdom and spiritual awareness. By aligning with a higher state of consciousness, individuals can break free from limiting beliefs and step into their full mental and emotional potential.

As we look at the future of wellness, alternative medicine offers a path to deeper integration of mind, body, and spirit. Expanding our awareness and embracing new healing modalities can help us align more fully with our soul's purpose.

REAL POWER IS TO BE FREE

When we begin to see ourselves as vessels of divine potential, we understand that our spirit and self-expression carry profound influence. By releasing fear and surrendering the need for control, we allow our authentic selves to emerge—uninhibited, grounded, and powerful.

Tapping into this deeper level of expression requires conscious awareness. With greater power comes greater responsibility—not just to ourselves, but to how we move through the world. When your internal state is aligned—your values, intentions, and energy—there's a natural flow. The universe responds to that integrity with support and synchronicity.

There are countless energies in the universe that uplift and support human growth. Among them are:

- Positive Energy – the fuel of optimism and possibility.

- Enthusiastic Energy – the drive that ignites action and forward motion.

- Euphoric Energy – the high vibration of joy and alignment.

- Pure Expressive Energy – the power to create without fear or restraint.

- Compassion – the bridge that connects us to others in understanding.

- Kindness – the simple, yet transformative force that softens hearts and fosters unity.

Harnessing these energies isn't about control, it is about resonance. When we align with them, we elevate ourselves and those around us.

.

SELF CONFIDENCE

If your child is facing bullying—whether at school or in the community—it's a deeply unsettling experience, not only for them but for you as a parent. These situations often involve complex social dynamics. Bullies tend to prey on those they perceive as vulnerable, as it offers them a sense of control or superiority. As a parent, your role is crucial in helping your child navigate this experience and regain their personal power.

While addressing bullying can be emotionally charged and even intimidating, it's worth considering the long-term benefits of guiding your child to assert themselves with confidence. Standing up to a bully doesn't guarantee the problem will end immediately, but it often shifts the dynamic. Bullies are less likely to continue their behavior when they're no longer met with fear or passivity. More importantly, the act of standing up for oneself can be a powerful catalyst for personal growth.

The confidence a child builds through self-advocacy often spills over into other areas of life. It helps them develop a more resilient mindset, improves their ability to manage stress, and contributes to stronger emotional well-being. Studies show that confident children are more likely to engage in positive self-talk, enjoy better physical health, and are less susceptible to anxiety or depression.

Fostering a mindset grounded in optimism and self-respect can be transformative. It allows your child to push past fear, embrace challenges, and expand their worldview. This shift in perspective can spark new interests, build stronger relationships, and create opportunities they might not have otherwise pursued.

Ultimately, helping your child find the strength to face bullying isn't just about addressing a momentary conflict. It is about equipping them with tools to empower them for a lifetime. It's a step toward building a strong, capable individual prepared to take on the world with confidence and clarity.

SPIRITUAL AWARENESS

Spirituality unfolds in layers as one journeys deeper into the path of enlightenment. At its foundation is the *structural-behaviorist approach*, which emphasizes behaviors and rituals that foster a sense of purpose, hope, and connection with God and His teachings. This form of spirituality is often rooted in established religious traditions and provides individuals with a framework to navigate life through meaning and moral grounding.

On a more advanced level is the *transcendent approach*, which focuses on transpersonal and intrapersonal transcendence. A profound sense of peace, unity, and harmony with the universe marks this type of spiritual experience. It can serve as a profound personal resource in emotional, psychological, or existential need.

Reaching this level of consciousness may seem abstract at first, but it's accessible. A helpful starting point is engaging with New Age spiritual literature. This genre bridges ancient religious wisdom with contemporary ideas of limitless possibility and divine potential. It reinforces the belief that the mind, when aligned with a higher power, can manifest healing, expansion, and insight beyond what was previously imagined.

As you explore these teachings, take time for contemplation. Reflection is a powerful practice that aligns your thought patterns with the greater intelligence of the universe. This mental and spiritual alignment can bring profound calm and clarity. One of the key outcomes of such inner work is the integration of the **mind, body, and spirit**, which generates internal harmony. Spiritual energy, when directed intentionally, supports emotional balance, boosts mental resilience, and can even contribute to physical well-being.

Spirituality, at its core, is a uniquely human endeavor. It is the pursuit of meaning beyond the self—a connection to others, nature, and a Supreme Being. Whether grounded in traditional faith or informed by New Age perspectives, the path invites us to seek truth, heal, and live with a deeper sense of purpose.

SPIRITUAL CLEANLINESS

Spiritual cleanliness is important because it represents inner purity, free from negative thoughts and actions, creating space for a deeper connection with oneself, a higher power, and fostering positive mental and emotional well-being. This practice often involves meditation, reflection, and actively working to cultivate good intentions and moral conduct, which helps maintain balance and promotes personal growth across various spiritual traditions.

If you've ever visited a monastery or convent, you've likely seen monks and nuns going about their daily tasks, many of which involve cleaning their sacred spaces. This is more than just about tidying up—it symbolizes clarity and organization. The universe, after all, was created with such precision and order by God, not through chaotic bursts of energy. It operates with incredible efficiency, perfect timing, and a sense of balance. This offers a powerful lesson on how to manage our own lives—with clarity, responsibility, and purpose.

Both outer and inner cleanliness are foundational to spiritual practice. Just as the monk or nun's broom touches the ground in a mindful way, it symbolizes a sacred relationship with Mother

Earth. We, too, need to create a space for ourselves that honors the sacredness both within us and in the world around us.

It's essential to take responsibility for our own spiritual growth and ask ourselves whether this is an area where we can improve. Spiritual development is about reflection and self-improvement. Life becomes much more interesting when we embrace trial and error as part of the journey. As long as we use reflection as a tool for growth and remain committed to self-improvement, each day becomes an opportunity for a new beginning.

THE SYNERGY OF TRIAL AND ERROR

We often face many peaks and valleys as we navigate through various periods of our lives. Occasionally when we are in the throes of the valleys, it is important to align yourself to God's superlatives and his divine Universe. The divine Universe is designed to assist mankind to help adjust his frame of mind through surrender, contemplation and prayer.

God's Universal Values include assisting and igniting one's life with commitment to positioning thoughts toward a more positive outlook.

"Success is the sum of many things done well," according to Bob Casey, Founder of UPS. Let's examine this quote more carefully. As you're moving towards your objective for success, the synergy of trial and error and reflection is the most potent energy you possess to reach your objective. But, to make this work, you have to put in the energy and the force of trial and error will take over.

In my opinion, when you begin an entrepreneurial venture, there are certain principles that will help you flourish. For example, being a businessperson that is committed to involvement in the local community and, if possible, giving some of your proceeds to those in need.

Deepak Chopra once said "An entrepreneur is somebody willing to take a risk to actualize their vision. I've envisioned a more peaceful, just, sustainable, healthy, and joyful world for thirty years. And I take an interest in only those areas."

With the hectic pace of life, it is important to have an organized methodology that encourages healthy repetition to fuel one's efforts to meet one's goals.

THE IMPACT OF TIME ON HUMANITY

Over 5,000 years ago, the Sumerians, one of the earliest known civilizations, revolutionized how humanity perceives and measures time. Residing in the region between the Tigris and Euphrates rivers—known as Mesopotamia—they developed the sexagesimal system, dividing the day into 24 hours, each hour into 60 minutes, and each minute into 60 seconds. This system was rooted in their advanced astronomical observations and the practical needs of their society. The number 60 was chosen due to its divisibility, allowing for precise timekeeping essential for agriculture, trade, and religious practices. Their innovations laid the foundation for the timekeeping systems we use today.

While the Sumerians gave us the structure of time, the human mind can transcend it. Through mental time travel, we can access memories from the past and envision possibilities for the future. This capability is not just a passive reflection but an active process where our thoughts generate electrical impulses that traverse the brain at speeds up to 270 miles per hour, effectively allowing us to move through time within our consciousness.

The brain's adaptability, known as neuroplasticity, is central to this phenomenon. Neuroplasticity refers to the brain's ability to reorganize itself by forming new neural connections throughout life. This process enables us to learn new skills, adapt to new experiences, and recover from injuries. Engaging in activities that challenge the brain, such as learning a new language or practicing mindfulness, can stimulate neuroplasticity, improving cognitive function and emotional resilience.

In essence, while the Sumerians provided us with the tools to measure time, our minds grant us the power to transcend it. Understanding and harnessing the brain's capacity for growth and adaptation allows us to navigate life's challenges and opportunities with greater awareness and purpose.

WHAT IS NORMAL?

As we journey through the practice of positive thinking, one essential principle is to withhold judgment of others. We often hear the question, "What is normal?" Dr. David Gupta offers a thoughtful perspective—what if the person we're judging is simply living in alignment with their own version of normal? His view is that each person defines their own standards, shaped by personal experiences, values, and identity. When we recognize this, we're reminded that everyone deserves the freedom to live authentically, free from imposed expectations.

When imagination connects with our inner spark, it can unleash a powerful current of positivity—not just within ourselves, but across our interactions and communities.

Throughout history, the idea of "normal" has been continually challenged by transformative thinkers and leaders. Figures like Jesus of Nazareth, Galileo Galilei, and Albert Einstein broke away from the norms of their time, shifting entire worldviews in the process.

Jesus taught radical forgiveness, love, and spiritual equality— teachings that reshaped human consciousness and laid the foundation for Christianity. Galileo dared to speak scientific truth in the face of religious dogma, asserting that the Earth revolved around the sun—an idea that led to his persecution. Einstein redefined the way we understand space and time, offering a theory of relativity that transformed modern physics.

Each of them defied societal norms not for the sake of rebellion, but to elevate human understanding. They were unapologetically themselves—and in doing so, they changed the world.

The timeless advice to "be yourself" remains as relevant as ever. Your unique voice, energy, and perspective matter. When you allow your authentic self to shine, you not only honor your own journey but also give others permission to do the same.

THE IMPORTANCE OF PRAYER

You can turn to prayer for many reasons—whether you're feeling grateful, struggling with depression, seeking healing, or navigating difficult moments. The power of prayer lies in its consistency and in your ability to follow through with actions that align with your requests.

When you ask for guidance from God, the key is to trust that divine wisdom will lead you toward a clearer path. It's about surrendering your needs and having faith that this trust will bring positive change to your life.

Prayer is most impactful when it becomes a regular practice—ideally, several times a week. In times of hardship, struggle, and sacrifice, remember that God's blessings often come when we persist, showing resilience and dedication. Over time, these efforts are recognized, and they create space for God's grace to flow more freely into our lives.

When we pray, whether to God, Jesus, or whatever higher power we believe in, we are petitioning for change, asking for guidance and assistance in manifesting what we seek. But it's not just about asking, it's also about reflecting on what needs to shift within us to receive those blessings.

Through prayer, we invite God to work through us, illuminating not only our lives but also those around us. It's a channel for growth, connection, and enlightenment.

Repenting for past actions is a powerful part of spiritual growth. True repentance—rooted in love and faith in God—can be done through personal reflection or with the guidance of clergy. This act of perfect contrition, where you acknowledge your mistakes and seek forgiveness, helps clear the path for divine healing and spiritual renewal.

THE MEANING OF RESILIENCE

Resilience in challenging times is an invaluable trait that amplifies our ability to persevere and keep moving forward. As the poet Emerson wisely said, "Whilst he sits on the cushion of advantages, he goes to sleep. When he is pushed, tormented, he has a chance to learn something." Embracing life's challenges and recognizing that we have the capacity to face whatever comes our way is empowering. Knowledge, ultimately, is the antidote to fear.

Adopting a positive outlook on life is crucial. While it takes effort, the rewards of maintaining optimism are immense and can profoundly impact our well-being. When setbacks arise, the key is to view them as opportunities for growth. Every setback offers a chance to reassess, learn, and move forward with more wisdom and experience. What might seem like an obstacle is often just a stepping stone in disguise, helping us become more well-rounded individuals.

This mindset shifts how we approach life, encouraging personal growth by reprogramming our brain to adapt and expand through new experiences. But for this transformation to happen, we must actively cultivate a positive attitude and embrace life's challenges head-on.

When we take bold steps forward, decisions that come from the core of our being, we are fueled by an inner strength that propels us toward our goals.

Resilience isn't a fixed trait. It's something we can all develop. It's about adopting behaviors, thoughts, and actions that strengthen us, enabling anyone to cultivate greater resilience over time.

THE POWER OF TRUTH

When we are driven by the power of truth, many hidden aspects of reality are unveiled. For example, information cannot remain concealed for long—it has a way of surfacing when it is propelled by truth's force.

Living with a sense of kindness and authenticity allows us to cultivate qualities that shape how others perceive our integrity. This, ultimately, is our greatest value, as it pays the richest dividends over time. The key is to embrace continuous learning and growth, using trial and error as a guide to measure progress.

Facing your fears is crucial, as it frees you from self-imposed limitations and allows you to expand beyond what your mind thought was possible. Once you tap into the full potential of your mind, the possibilities in the material world are limitless. With belief, nothing is out of reach.

It's essential to have a clear vision of how you want to live your life, allowing that direction to propel you toward enlightenment, while staying true to your authentic self. When you find inner harmony, you align with both your purpose and your Divine Source, guiding yourself toward a life filled with meaning.

As you embark on discovering your purpose, it's vital to trust your intuition—it will be your compass along the way. Hustle, paired with the right mindset, will propel you toward your goals. But hustle isn't just about hard work; it's about believing in yourself and your ability to achieve greatness. The right thoughts allow you to venture into uncharted territory, revealing opportunities beyond your wildest imagination.

THE SPIRITUAL AGE OF AQUARIUS

Astrologers suggest that the movement of celestial bodies influences not only individual lives, but also the cultural and societal development of humanity. We are transitioning from the Age of Pisces, where our primary focus was on understanding our identity and existence, into the Age of Aquarius, which is characterized by a collective pursuit of peace and unity. This shift is not just a concept—it is already impacting individuals and societies and it will continue to shape our future.

The lessons passed down by previous generations, grounded in the Piscean age, are now being reassessed. In the Age of Aquarius, we are called to move away from old paradigms and embrace a more enlightened perspective. We are being urged to accept that we no longer need to place our beliefs in anything external to ourselves. Everything within us, and everything in the universe, is a reflection of the divine—God, in its purest form. To align with God and achieve unity and balance, we must recognize that this divine force expresses itself both within us and in the world around us.

In this new era, the idea of pantheism has gained prominence, suggesting that the universe itself embodies divine energy. The New Age movement embraces this concept, blending ancient spiritual teachings with modern ideas. Followers believe that God and the universe are inseparable, with divine energy permeating every aspect of existence, offering humanity the opportunity for growth and expansion on both personal and collective levels.

THE TRUTH IS THE TRUTH

The truth is an unstoppable force, inherently tied to universal laws and principles that govern time and existence. No matter how much we might try to suppress it, the truth will always emerge—sometimes subtly and sometimes with undeniable clarity. Its momentum is a constant, and when the time is right, it reveals itself in various forms.

Looking through history, we can see countless sacrifices made to bring the truth to light. These sacrifices often come with a profound sense of purpose, and there are larger, universal forces at play that support this revelation. It's a complex network of actions, events, and divine forces that work together to ensure the truth surfaces when it needs to.

Consider the signers of the Declaration of Independence. Many of them endured great personal sacrifice for their beliefs, yet they stood firm in their commitment to a greater truth: that all men are created equal. Their willingness to endure hardship for this cause exemplifies how truth is often linked to great personal cost but ultimately propels society forward.

Living a life guided by principles can lead to moments of challenge and sacrifice, but it's important to remember that these trials are part of the process. As you move through difficulties, the truth will reveal itself in ways that reinforce your convictions, bringing light and clarity even in the darkest of times. Truth and principles are intertwined, and they often surface with a sense of love, conviction, and purpose.

As you grow older, it becomes essential to reevaluate your priorities and focus on your potential. Embrace who you are and what you are capable of achieving, striving toward your fullest potential. However, it's vital to remember that no one achieves greatness alone—we all need guidance, both from within and from higher sources.

The Universe is Within Us

The universe operates on the principle that every action has a corresponding effect. This means that every energy we put out—whether positive or negative—can have a profound impact on our lives. The energy we contribute to the world flows back to us, shaping our reality in ways we often don't fully understand.

It all begins with intention. When your intentions are rooted in goodness and integrity, you align yourself with positive forces, which in turn enhances your Karma and can lead to greater manifestations in your life. Intentions have power— they shape not just your actions, but the outcomes you attract.

The universe and our own existence are intricately linked. The same atoms, protons, and electrons that make up the universe also compose our bodies. Understanding the forces at play within us—through self-awareness and growth— helps us nurture our well-being and create harmony within.

The universe is a powerful partner in turning ideas into reality. By learning how it functions, you can work in harmony with its natural flow to bring your goals to fruition. When you understand the components that make up existence, you can harness those forces to manifest your desires.

To align yourself with the universe's energy, it is essential to practice meditation or deep contemplation on the spiritual material that resonates with you. This practice helps you tune into the universal forces, which can guide you in achieving your aspirations.

Once you've mapped out your plan and set your intentions, the next step is to cross that threshold and transform your ideas into tangible actions. It's crucial to allow love to lead the way. When you approach life with unconditional love—free of expectations and driven solely by pure intention—you open yourself to true enlightenment and the limitless potential that comes with it.

TRANSFORMATION

Turmoil and transformation are often intertwined. During times of struggle or hardship, many people naturally turn to prayer. Prayer is a powerful tool because, in many spiritual traditions, it is believed that God understands the innermost thoughts and emotions of our hearts. It is a way of connecting with the divine and setting the stage for the changes you seek in your life.

Prayer is more than just asking for help—it's a request for guidance, support, and alignment with your higher purpose. It's a way to activate your desires through faith, seeking the divine intervention needed to bring those desires to fruition.

To receive the grace that God offers, it's essential to reflect on the areas of your life where change is needed. If you find yourself regretting past actions, this can be a moment to deepen your faith and increase your love for God. This process, known as Perfect Contrition, involves repentance, which can be done in a place of quiet reflection, either with a clergy member or in solitude, treating your mind as a temple for introspection.

As you explore self-help resources or spiritual teachings, remember that God understands your struggles. Through contemplation and prayer, divine blessings will gradually support and guide you through your challenges, offering comfort and wisdom.

The more you engage in prayer and reflection, and invite God's presence into your life, the more you'll begin to feel the divine calling to walk a path of enlightenment. This journey will inspire subtle shifts in your behavior, allowing you to detach from distractions and unhealthy attachments. While God's support is crucial, personal effort remains key. With faith and divine guidance, you can consciously work towards transforming your life.

Many individuals have undergone profound transformations by walking this path of enlightenment. May you find strength, peace, and clarity along your own journey. Godspeed.

TRUE NORTH

In spiritual terms, "true north" represents a fixed point of guidance, symbolizing a person's highest values, core beliefs, or a divine source that serves as an internal compass. It's a reference that offers direction during life's decisions and challenges, much like how the North Star guided travelers for centuries. "True north" helps keep us aligned with our authentic selves, allowing us to stay true to our purpose even when external distractions or conflicting viewpoints try to sway us.

Here are key points about the concept of "true north" in spirituality:

Inner Compass: "True north" is an internal guide, not something external. It's about understanding what is right and true for you. This inner compass is crucial as it reflects your personal values, your sense of purpose, and your authentic self.

It's vital to engage in self-reflection, analyzing both your strengths and weaknesses. This will help you create a path forward, one that is grounded in prayer and guided by wisdom as you move towards enlightenment.

Divine Connection: In various spiritual traditions, "true north" is often connected to a higher power—be it God, the Universe, or another divine source. It represents the direction to seeking spiritual growth, aligning your life with divine principles.

Spirituality, in its many forms, can be transformative. Its teachings can inspire and guide you toward fulfillment, helping you navigate life with a clearer sense of purpose.

Staying on Course: Just as a compass always points north, your "true north" ensures you stay on course. It helps you navigate life's complexities, constantly reminding you of your core values and guiding you towards decisions that reflect your highest good.

Symbiotic Journey: We, as humans, need to recognize the interconnectedness of all people. Our paths toward our individual "true north" are not isolated; we share common experiences, challenges, and goals with others. In this shared journey, we can support each other, creating a symbiotic bond that strengthens our collective pursuit of purpose.

VIBRATIONAL CONSCIOUSNESS

What does it mean to raise your vibrational consciousness? As you continue your spiritual journey, you begin to receive divine blessings. Within these blessings is vibrational energy that drives your spiritual ascension, a process of moving toward a higher state of awareness and growth. Spiritual ascension is about transcending your current state and stepping into a more enlightened existence. It often means gaining a deeper understanding of God's plan and your role within it, leading to personal transformation. This journey is viewed across many spiritual traditions as a metaphorical rise to a more elevated state of being.

As you engage with spiritual teachings, you elevate your connection with God. The process of reading, reflecting, and contemplating spiritual content deepens your worship and connection. The more you immerse yourself in these teachings, the more God reciprocates with blessings that empower your personal growth. Through this process, you are gradually transformed. However, it's important to remember that as you walk this path, you must stay focused on your priorities. God's transformative work in your life requires both commitment and action—what you invest in your spiritual journey, God amplifies in return.

Living a principled life is essential because the principles you uphold reflect who you are and who you aspire to become. Principles have immense power—just as Patrick Henry's famous declaration, "Give me liberty, or give me death," became a rallying cry that inspired a nation. Living by principles can inspire those around you in ways you may never fully understand, creating a ripple effect of positive influence. By demonstrating your values consistently, you become a living example of the power of integrity and faith.

WHAT IS A PURPOSEFUL LIFE?

As I delved into this topic, I encountered many insights that offered valuable perspectives. What does it mean to live a purposeful life? A purposeful life is one that aligns with your true, authentic self and harmonizes with the Divine Universe. When you find your "happy place" and feel content, you are in tune with your inner being, your thoughts, and your connection to the divine.

In the early stages of discovering your purpose, it's important to listen to your intuition. Your intuition acts as a compass, guiding you along your path. In addition to intuition, having a clear vision and a determined work ethic will drive you toward your goals. Hustle is about believing in your potential and pushing forward to achieve your highest aspirations.

Take, for example, the Founding Fathers of our country. They studied scripture and philosophical principles to shape their vision of liberty, life, and the pursuit of happiness. At the time, there was no government like the one they were trying to create—a system based on unprecedented ideals. While it's not a perfect system, it remains one of the most robust frameworks for governance in the world today. It all started with a powerful sense of purpose.

As you move forward in life, it's crucial to focus your energy on a singular vision. Spreading yourself too thin can dilute your efforts and slow progress. By channeling your energy into one clear goal, you solidify your efforts and see quicker, more substantial results. The mind, when empowered with belief, is an incredibly potent tool for shaping your future.

WHAT IS BEAUTIFUL?

Beauty is subjective, with many ways to appreciate it, whether it's through nature, art, music, or the unique qualities of someone's personality. But what part of the brain helps us recognize beauty? The orbitofrontal cortex, located in the brain, plays a key role in how we perceive and enjoy beauty. At its core, beauty is about our ability to connect with and appreciate what we find admirable in the world around us.

Interestingly, exposure to nature's beauty can have lasting effects on our well-being. Research shows that people who are regularly exposed to nature not only experience increased happiness and enthusiasm but also benefit physically. Nature can enhance our physiological health and make us more open to positive energy.

The power of nature's impact is so significant that it has been studied in various medical settings, particularly regarding patient recovery times. One study, for example, found that patients in hospitals who had rooms with windows looking out onto trees and natural landscapes had significantly better recovery outcomes than those whose rooms faced brick walls.

Nurses recorded an average of four negative comments per patient who had no nature view, such as "needs encouragement" or "upset and crying." In contrast, patients with nature views received far fewer negative notes—only one during their entire stay. These patients were otherwise very similar, and had received the same treatment, so the only variable was the natural view.

This study highlights how nature's beauty can impact not just our mood, but our health. Whether it's the calming effect of a natural scene or the restorative power of greenery, nature offers countless benefits for the mind, body, and spirit.

Boldness

As you navigate through life, many people fail to tap into their abstract abilities, which have the power to shift their dynamics and propel them forward. By embracing boldness instead of playing it safe, you're taking a crucial step in believing in yourself. Boldness empowers you to cultivate positive self-talk, reinforcing your willpower to overcome obstacles and achieve your goals.

Every investment of positive energy you make is never wasted. Words stem from thoughts, and those thoughts hold the power to transform our intentions. One core aspect of faith is believing in the impossible. Faith isn't just about believing in your own capabilities. It is also about trusting in something greater than yourself, a higher spiritual power.

When we think about universal energy, we often picture particles, photons, and atoms—all the building blocks of the universe. In this context, the mind must recognize its ability to bridge the gap between perception and the abstract thinking required to harness that energy. By focusing on belief rather than doubt, you open yourself to the flow of universal energy. It's in this space that we create awareness and can overcome seemingly insurmountable challenges, because, while the path may be tough, it offers the richest lessons when we choose to embrace it.

WHAT IS "REAL" POWER?

When we consider the universe, it's clear that energy manifests in many forms. The way we direct and invest our energy is crucial because different levels of radiance emerge from the universe. Positive thoughts, for example, are lighter frequencies that carry reinforcing, uplifting energy, helping to propel us forward in life. In contrast, negative thoughts are heavier frequencies, pulling us down and clouding our minds with cynicism and pessimism.

What truly opens our consciousness and allows us to experience freedom is when we allow ourselves to express our authentic persona. This authenticity breaks us free from societal expectations and allows us to reach our true potential. One of the greatest tests of true power lies in staying true to your principles when confronted with your greatest fears.

Let's consider the concept of true power. In his book The Seat of the Soul, Gary Zukav argues that power is not about imposing your will on others. Fear, no matter how fortified, does not equate to power. For example, the vast armies of Rome have long since faded, yet the life and teachings of a single man, put to death by those same soldiers, continue to shape the course of humanity today. So, who truly possessed power?

What is Suffering?

Suffering often arises when we engage in actions that aren't aligned with our core principles. We can contribute to our own pain by fostering unhealthy patterns of thought that emerge in response to discomfort. These thoughts, rooted in pain, create artificial attachments that typically lead to more suffering. However, once we recognize this dynamic, we can begin the journey toward healing and wholeness.

Understanding suffering can be the catalyst for personal awakening. Once we acknowledge it, we open the door to self-reflection and healing. There are various methods to heal from suffering, including:

- Prayer

- Meditation

- Reading spiritual or enlightening content

- Contemplation

The key to achieving lasting happiness lies in committing to the enlightened path. This commitment strengthens us, helping our minds expand, reducing fear, and building momentum toward a more fulfilling life.

Finding one's purpose is essential, and it starts with tuning into your intuition. Pay attention to your inner voice. Positive thoughts, once they enter your pre-frontal cortex, are sent out to the universe, aligning with what you need and helping manifest your desires.

Setting clear objectives can become a self-fulfilling prophecy. By consciously shaping our actions and mindset, we influence future outcomes. Let's embrace life fully and open ourselves to the infinite possibilities that tomorrow holds.

YOU GET WHAT YOU ACCEPT

The principle behind the phrase "You get what you accept" reflects a universal cycle, one that emphasizes the importance of continuous growth and avoiding complacency in life. If you adopt the mindset that your rewards are directly tied to the effort you put in, you will keep moving forward, consistently finding new opportunities. This perspective transforms how you see life, as it constantly evolves and challenges you to grow. Think of it like standing atop a mountain, where you can look back at the path you've traveled and ahead to what lies in the distance. The journey you've taken becomes an essential part of how you prepare for future challenges, providing valuable insight into how to approach your goals.

Human history is a testament to our ability to innovate and create. From the invention of the wheel to the discovery of electricity and the advent of technologies like smartphones, our progress has been fueled by our creativity and drive to improve. These breakthroughs have reshaped our world and continuously pushed us forward.

At the heart of this progress lies the unique human capacity— the determination, willpower, and ambition that propel us to exceed limits and accomplish the extraordinary. Our evolution has been driven by our quest to conquer fear and expand our understanding. This relentless pursuit of growth remains key to unlocking our full potential and realizing the highest expression of who we are meant to be.

INSIGHTS FROM THE MASTERS

Saint Ignatius of Loyola taught us the significance of living with joy, love, and a commitment to service. He encouraged us to praise God, trust in the power of prayer, and ask for what we need. Reflecting on our actions, he believed, is a vital practice in shaping our character and strengthening our connection to the divine. St. Ignatius advocated for finding God's presence in every aspect of our lives, maintaining an optimistic outlook, and practicing gratitude. By keeping a joyful attitude while seeking God's grace, he believed we would experience real transformation and growth.

Eckhart Tolle, author of The Power of Now, offers a philosophy centered on transcending the ego and aligning with our true essence. He emphasizes the importance of being present, free from the distractions of mental noise, and connecting with the stillness within. Tolle argues that true happiness and fulfillment are found in the present moment, not by dwelling on past regrets or worrying about the future.

Master Choa Kok Sui, Former Guru of the Pranic Healing Institute and a modern spiritual teacher, focused his life's work on understanding how energy affects our overall well-being. He teaches that our primary goal is to improve our health and vitality, not just for ourselves but for the benefit of those around us. According to Master Choa, well-being is far more than just the absence of illness—it encompasses physical, emotional, mental, financial, and spiritual health. He emphasizes that we are the sum of our thoughts, actions, and decisions. Since our thoughts shape our experiences, it is crucial to be mindful of them, as they influence not only our lives but also the world around us.

A Healthier You

The human body is an extraordinary creation, showcasing the complexity and brilliance of nature's design. One fascinating aspect of our biology is how our sensory system helps us recognize when we're nourishing ourselves with healthy food and drink. When we consume wholesome options like orange juice, apple juice, green tea, cranberry juice, cantaloupe, honeydew, bananas, blueberries, or cashews, our bodies respond positively, signaling to the brain that we're receiving beneficial nutrients. This mind-body connection highlights the importance of what we put into our bodies, reinforcing the idea that our choices matter.

A critical component of this process is the cardiovascular system, which includes the heart and a network of blood vessels working together to circulate blood throughout the body. Keeping this system healthy should be a top priority since it's essential for overall well-being. One major threat to cardiovascular health comes from free radicals—unstable molecules in the bloodstream that can damage cells and contribute to a range of health issues, including heart disease, respiratory problems, and even cancer. Free radicals can also accelerate the aging process.

Thankfully, there are several ways to mitigate the damage caused by free radicals. A diet rich in antioxidants can neutralize these harmful molecules. Foods like berries, leafy greens, and nuts are great sources of antioxidants. Additionally, supplements such as turmeric with curcumin and CoQ10 offer antioxidant benefits and can support heart health. However, it's important to consult a healthcare professional before adding any new supplements to your regimen.

In the end, the complexity and beauty of the human body are a testament to nature's genius. By understanding how our bodies function and how to support them with healthy choices, we empower ourselves to improve our well-being. Making informed, mindful decisions about our health leads to a higher quality of life and greater vitality.

NEVER GIVE UP

Dark forces have existed throughout human history, constantly working to undermine our progress. These forces often manifest as negative emotions and behaviors—such as jealousy, bitterness, hatred, pride, and judgment. Understanding that these harmful traits are fueled by darker energies can help us realize that they aim to prevent us from reaching our full potential. The key to overcoming these destructive influences starts with self-awareness. By recognizing these fears and negative patterns within us, we can begin to take steps toward healing, seeking guidance from a higher power through prayer and reflection.

One of the most powerful ways to regain control of our lives is to focus on the divine qualities of love, peace, forgiveness, hope, courage, and faith. These principles act as a counterbalance to the negativity that can cloud our thoughts and actions. No matter where we are in life or what obstacles we face, embracing these qualities gives us the strength to overcome—even when the road ahead seems impossible. The forces of good, fueled by hope and belief, can ignite profound transformation in our lives, but it all begins with our commitment to shift our energy in a positive direction.

This message is for everyone—whether you are deeply spiritual or an atheist. Regardless of your beliefs, we all share this world, and we all have the potential for growth and change. Hope has the unique ability to inspire courage, and that courage can lead us back to a place of positivity and light.

The universe encourages us to look inward, confront our challenges, and surrender our needs through prayer. Life on Earth is an opportunity to grow, evolve, and strive toward becoming the best versions of ourselves. As we move forward, let's embrace the promise of a brighter future, always striving to improve and honor our journey toward enlightenment.

KEY TAKE-AWAYS ON LIFE

To truly live life to the fullest, we must learn to do so without fear. Fear holds us back, limiting our growth and potential. We unlock our ability to expand and reach new heights when we overcome fear. One of the ways to challenge fear is by engaging with positive, empowering content, which broadens our minds and nurtures creativity. With this mindset, we can think expansively and innovate in ways that are only possible when we are free from fear.

This is the way God's Universe works.

Pray to God for Guidance

Supreme God,

"Guide me, God, as I explore the vastness of my mind. Help me believe that I can move mountains with my thoughts and abilities. Allow me to break beyond my current limits and realize my true potential. Lead me to think and wonder with boundless imagination to create new ideas that are only possible when I am free of fear."

Status Quo

To unleash your true potential, it is crucial to both work within the system and challenge it. We can conquer the forces of fear by liberating our minds and daring to explore beyond the limits of what we know. It's our responsibility to pursue this journey with courage and calculated risk. Fear will always try to suppress us, but we have the power to release old constraints and embrace new ideas. Challenging the status quo—even within our own comfort zones—is necessary for achieving our highest success.

What is Real Power?

As Gary Zukav explains in Seat of the Soul, true power isn't about imposing our will on others. There is no real power in fear, even when it's backed by force. The Roman Empire's military power dissolved centuries ago, but the impact of the life and death of a single man continues to shape humanity. Who, then, had true power?

Repetition

When we consistently invest energy into our goals, we spark new vitality and connect our efforts with positive energy. This cycle of repetition creates an energetic link between hard work and personal growth—between the actions we take and the energy we generate. By sustaining this energy, we elevate ourselves and push forward toward the highest achievements.

Vibration

There are countless lessons to learn from the Divine Universe. One of the most significant is understanding the constant vibration that permeates everything. Everything in the universe vibrates at a frequency, with energy moving at the most fundamental level of matter. The ancient Greek philosophers pondered how matter could be broken down into even smaller particles—atoms—that would vibrate at the most basic level. It's at this foundational level that healing begins, starting with the cells in our bodies.

Snowflake

Just as no two snowflakes are alike, each one unique in its design and structure, we too are part of the vast, interconnected universe. Snowflakes are a microcosm of God's divine design—a symbol of His majesty, where His power and creation are reflected in every unique thing. This speaks to the infinite beauty of God's sovereignty over the universe He created.

Tomorrow

As we look ahead to tomorrow, we're reminded that life naturally unfolds with positive, forward-moving energy. Each new day is a built-in opportunity for renewal. When we make mistakes, we can count on the sun rising again, bringing with it the chance to let go of the past and focus our energy on the possibilities of the new day. This continuous cycle gives us the strength to keep going and evolve as we pursue life's purpose.

Believing in the Impossible

The mind is a powerful force, and when we truly learn to tap into it, we begin to understand just how limitless our potential really is. Once you unleash the full capacity of your thoughts and imagination, the material world—no matter how vast—becomes secondary to what you believe you can achieve. When belief becomes the driving force behind your actions, the concept of "impossible" loses all meaning. The mind, empowered by faith and intention, can break through any boundary.

Confidence

True confidence is forged through perseverance. It's not about avoiding failure, but learning through the process of trial, error, and honest reflection. When we evaluate our actions with clarity and adjust as needed, we strengthen our belief in our abilities. Facing life's biggest challenges with courage builds resilience. As Deepak Chopra puts it, "Whatever you project will come back to you"—meaning your internal narrative will ultimately shape your external reality.

What Is a Positive Paradigm Shift?

A paradigm shift is a transformative change in perspective—one that alters how you approach life, decision-making, and problem-solving. These shifts often arise when new ideas or experiences challenge old patterns of thought. For example, the invention of the smartphone created a global paradigm shift—redefining how we communicate, shop, socialize, and even think. In a personal context, a positive paradigm shift can redefine your mindset, habits, and goals, leading to lasting change and growth.

Embracing Love to Overcome Fear

Fear diminishes when love becomes the driving force of our energy. By praying and worshiping, we align ourselves with divine love, which reciprocates and limits fear. This universal law suggests that the more love we project, the more we receive, creating a cycle that diminishes fear.

Cultivating Consciousness

Caroline Myss, a renowned medical intuitive, teaches that when someone irritates you, it's important to recognize that they are operating at their highest level of consciousness. This perspective encourages self-awareness and compassion, reminding us not to overreact but to understand the limitations others may be facing.

The Interconnectedness of Energy

Everything in the universe is interconnected through energy. When a person passes away under a tree and their matter decomposes into the soil, they become part of that tree. This illustrates how we are all part of the same fabric of the universe, connected through atoms, protons, electrons, and neutrons.

Harnessing Universal Energy

Universal energy exists in all things, manifesting as particles, photon energy, and atoms. Our minds have the ability to close the gap between perception and the energy generated by our thoughts. By investing energy into believing in the impossible, we can overcome challenges and learn from the opportunities they present.

The Power of Positive Thought

The way we invest our energy is crucial, as different energies radiate at varying frequencies. Positive thoughts emit lighter, reinforcing energy that propels us forward, while negative thoughts can weigh us down, leading to cynicism and negative thinking. Focusing on positive energy can transform our experiences and outlook on life.

Navigating Negativity with Grace

When surrounded by negativity, it's important to approach the situation with the right mindset. By waking up each day with the abundant power of possibilities and the objective of fulfilling our purpose, we can engage in negativity with grace and nobility, becoming examples of positivity and light.

Staying Centered Amidst Challenges

Negative individuals may attempt to pull us away from our center, where our authentic selves reside. It's essential to stay focused and disciplined, remaining at the heart of our center. Through prayer and maintaining our integrity, we can find peace and strength, even when faced with external negativity.

The Transformative Power of Love

Love is a cornerstone of spiritual growth. Divine love is abundant and purifying, cleansing everything in its path. As Dr. Wayne Dyer said, "Hate converts to love when the energy of love is in its presence." Embracing love allows us to transform negative emotions and experiences into opportunities for growth and healing.

The Majesty of Creation

Rainbows have been admired throughout history for their beauty and complexity. They serve as a reminder of the divine presence in all things, reflecting the majesty and creativity of the universe. Recognizing the wonder in natural phenomena can deepen our appreciation for the interconnectedness of all life.

Love Shapes Our Future

Love is a powerful investment in the belief that positive change is possible. By nurturing past connections and embracing love in all forms, we can transcend challenges and cultivate a deeper spiritual understanding. This intentional practice of love not only enriches our lives but also paves the way for a brighter future.

Trusting God

Seeking divine guidance begins with trust. Regular prayer and reflection help align our actions with our spiritual values. By creating an action plan that mirrors our prayers and staying attuned to our intuition, we can navigate life's journey with confidence. Embracing struggle and sacrifice as part of the process allows us to grow and fulfill our purpose. As we trust in God's plan, we find clarity and direction.

Treasures

Life's journey is marked by cycles of highs and lows. During challenging times, it's essential to recognize and cherish the simple joys that sustain us—be it a walk in the park, tending to a garden, or watching the sunrise. These moments of peace and gratitude help us build resilience and appreciate the values that guide us, preparing us for the brighter days ahead.

Laws of the Universe

Mathematics offers a lens through which we can understand the universe's laws. The Big Bang Theory, explained through algebra, calculus, and physics, suggests a structured origin of the cosmos. Yet, it's worth contemplating: could such an intricate design emerge without a divine plan? Only a higher power could position the Earth at the perfect distance from the Sun, allowing life to flourish.

Faced with an Obstacle

Obstacles are inevitable, but our response defines us. Instead of doubting ourselves, we can confront challenges with faith and determination. By aligning our actions with our beliefs and trusting in divine support, we can transform barriers into steppingstones. As Buddha wisely stated, "Our life is shaped by our minds; we become what we think."

Embracing Life's Journey

Viewing life as an adventure encourages us to approach each day with purpose and enthusiasm. Setting clear goals and creating a roadmap, such as a five-year plan, can help measure progress and keep us motivated. The focus should be on continuous growth, striving to elevate ourselves and maintain a positive trajectory.

The Power of Dreams

Dreams serve as a conduit for inspiration, offering insights and guidance. For instance, Paul McCartney's song "Let It Be" was inspired by a dream where his late mother comforted him with the words "let it be" during a challenging time. Such dreams can provide clarity and spark creativity.

Discovering Our Purpose

Our purpose unfolds through daily actions and reflections. Embracing each day with passion and learning from past experiences propels us toward fulfillment. Mistakes become stepping stones, helping us align with our true calling and advance in our personal and spiritual growth.

The Aquarius Mindset

The Aquarius mindset embodies unity with nature and the cosmos. This perspective encourages spiritual awakening and a deeper connection with the universe. Embracing this consciousness can lead to personal transformation and a greater understanding of our place in the world.

Transformation and Growth

Personal transformation is akin to the metamorphosis of a caterpillar into a butterfly. Letting go of limiting beliefs and attachments allows for spiritual renewal. This process opens our minds to new possibilities and fosters a deeper connection with our inner selves.

Vibration

On the journey toward spiritual growth, elevating your vibration becomes a vital part of the process. This can be cultivated through practices like meditation, immersing yourself in literature focused on mind, body, and spirit, and dedicating time for meaningful reflection. These intentional acts contribute to your spiritual ascension, allowing you to operate on a higher energetic frequency. Beginning each day with gratitude sets a powerful tone—it generates positive energy that flows outward and, in turn, draws blessings from God in response to your thankful heart.

Forgiveness

Forgiveness is not about excusing someone's wrongdoing; it's about releasing yourself from the emotional weight of resentment. Choosing to forgive is a conscious act of humility and spiritual surrender. By letting go of bitterness, you allow God to lift that burden and replace it with peace. True forgiveness liberates your spirit and aligns you with a higher state of emotional and spiritual well-being. It is one of the most powerful ways to begin healing and move forward with clarity.

Keys to Success

Success requires courage and a willingness to hold yourself accountable. It's about embracing both your achievements and your missteps without hesitation. Growth comes through taking risks, learning from failure, and continuing to pursue your goals with boldness. Playing it safe can dilute your potential, while calculated risks build resilience and open doors. Confidence and momentum are the results of perseverance—two essential traits that keep you aligned with your purpose and progressing toward your highest aspirations.

Love

God is the ultimate source of pure, unconditional love—the foundation of creation itself. Love unites us, uplifts us, and heals us. It is one of the universal forces that governs humanity and transcends time. Dr. Wayne Dyer once said, "Hate converts to Love when the energy of Love is in its presence." Love has the power to neutralize negativity and restore harmony. The love that comes from God is deeply transformational—it's a divine energy that flows through all things, sustaining life and inspiring compassion in us all.

Hills and Valleys

Life's journey is often described as a series of peaks and valleys. While it's easy to feel disheartened during challenging times, it's essential to remember that perseverance and resilience can turn adversity into opportunity. As Branch Rickey, a prominent baseball executive, once said, "Luck is the residue of design," emphasizing that success often results from intentional effort and planning rather than mere chance.

Total Harmony

Achieving balance requires integrating both the spiritual and physical aspects of our lives. By aligning our actions with our values and maintaining a mindful presence, we can foster a sense of harmony that supports our well-being and purpose.

Spirituality

The vastness of the universe invites reflection on our place within it. As Dr. Wayne Dyer noted, "Love is the most powerful and still the most unknown energy of the world," suggesting that embracing love and connection can lead to profound spiritual growth.

Ripples of Positive Energy

Maintaining a positive mindset can have far-reaching effects. Positive thoughts and actions create a ripple effect, influencing not only our immediate environment but also contributing to a collective uplift in global consciousness.

How to Reach a Level of Success

Success is often the culmination of consistent effort and a positive mindset. By setting clear goals, embracing challenges, and learning from experiences, we can pave the way toward achieving our aspirations.

Boldness

Many individuals hesitate to tap into their full potential, often choosing comfort over challenge. Embracing boldness means stepping out of your comfort zone and trusting in your abilities. It's about making intentional choices that align with your goals, even when the path is uncertain. By cultivating self-belief and maintaining a positive mindset, you empower yourself to navigate obstacles and achieve your aspirations.

What is Normal?

In our journey toward personal growth, it's essential to recognize that each person's "normal" is unique. Dr. David Gupta emphasizes that individuals operate based on their own standards and perceptions. Instead of judging others, we should embrace diversity and understand that everyone is navigating their own path. This perspective fosters empathy and encourages a more inclusive and supportive environment.

Being Hurt

Experiencing hurt is an inevitable part of life, but it's also an opportunity for growth. Instead of harboring resentment, consider seeking solace and guidance through prayer or reflection. This practice can help release negative emotions and pave the way for healing. By embracing love and compassion, you can transform pain into strength and move forward with a renewed sense of purpose.

To Be Free

In our pursuit of purpose, we are blessed with the freedom to worship and the opportunity to work diligently toward our goals. Celebrating our achievements and finding joy in daily tasks are integral to a fulfilling life. Equally important is maintaining a habit of prayer, seeking guidance and expressing gratitude regularly. These practices ground us, helping us navigate life's challenges with clarity and purpose.

Life's Cycles

Life is a series of cycles, each presenting opportunities for growth. When faced with negativity, we can reflect, reassess, and realign our goals. Prayer is a tool for introspection, helping us stay connected to our mission. By expanding our minds and embracing divine guidance, we can move forward with intention. As Buddha wisely said, "There are only two mistakes one can make along the road to truth; not going all the way, and not starting."

Come Alive

When feeling stagnant, it's essential to reignite our inner drive. Embracing the energy that comes from a higher source can propel us forward. God's love and abundance are ever-present, offering us the strength to face challenges. By practicing resilience and harnessing the power of prayer, we can manifest a brighter future and approach each day with renewed vigor.

What is Passion?

Passion is the fervor that fuels our endeavors, driving us to pursue goals with enthusiasm and determination. When combined with emotional intelligence and critical thinking, passion becomes a powerful force for achievement. This synergy enables us to overcome obstacles and reach new heights, turning aspirations into tangible successes.

Faith

Faith is the cornerstone that supports us during both triumphs and trials. A steadfast belief provides stability, allowing us to navigate life's uncertainties with confidence. It empowers us to transcend fears and negative emotions, fostering growth and resilience. By embracing faith, we honor our potential and align ourselves with a higher purpose.

Hope

Hope is the force that propels us forward, an infinite energy that mirrors the boundless nature of the universe. It is a reflection of God's love, transcending all limitations. The universe, a harmonious symphony of living energy, awaits our connection. Through practices like meditation and positive thinking, we align ourselves with this universal flow, inviting blessings and guidance into our lives.

Obstacles

Life's challenges are inevitable, but they are also opportunities for growth. Embracing each setback as a lesson allows us to build resilience. By taking consistent steps forward, we move closer to a brighter future. As Caroline Myss suggests, our souls reside in the present moment, offering insights that our minds alone may not perceive. Trusting this inner wisdom can lead us to overcome any obstacle.

Abundant Energy

The energy we seek is not external but resides within us, a divine force that connects all creation. This energy is limitless, capable of overcoming any barrier in its path. By tapping into this source, we align ourselves with God's purpose, manifesting strength and clarity in our endeavors.

Spiritual Thinking

In times of despair, turning inward can provide solace. Dr. Lisa Miller's research highlights the profound impact of spirituality on mental well-being. Spiritual practices, such as meditation and prayer, strengthen our resilience, reducing the risk of depression and anxiety. Nurturing our spiritual core fosters a sense of peace and purpose, guiding us through life's challenges.

Universe and Healing

We are not separate from the universe but an integral part of it. The same energy that flows through the cosmos circulates within us. Understanding this interconnectedness enhances our capacity for healing. By aligning with the universe's rhythm, we open ourselves to transformative energy that promotes well-being and growth.

Mind Expansion

The potential of the human mind is vast, capable of achieving what may seem impossible. As Jesus taught, faith even as small as a mustard seed can move mountains. By expanding our consciousness and embracing our divine connection, we unlock the power to transform our reality, realizing that our capabilities are as limitless as our faith.

Benchmarking Growth

Success doesn't come from shortcuts. It's built through trial, error, and reflection. Each misstep offers insights—consider them data points, not failures. By analyzing these experiences, you can establish benchmarks that inform you of your next steps. This iterative process transforms setbacks into strategic advantages, guiding you toward your goals with greater clarity.

The Limitless Mind

Your mind's capacity isn't confined by current circumstances. It's a dynamic force that thrives on curiosity, resilience, and purpose. While life's challenges are inevitable, your mindset determines how you navigate them. By fostering a growth-oriented perspective, you can expand your mental horizons and unlock new possibilities.

Embracing the Divine

At the core of existence lies a singular, unifying force—God. This divine presence transcends time and space, offering guidance and strength. By aligning with this higher power, you tap into a wellspring of wisdom and resilience, empowering you to face life's challenges with grace and confidence.

Calculated Risk

True progress often requires stepping into the unknown. However, success isn't about reckless abandon; it's about informed risk-taking. By assessing potential outcomes and preparing accordingly, you can navigate uncertainties with confidence. As Richard Harpin emphasizes, proactive risk management is crucial for growth and innovation.

Focused Energy

Energy is a finite resource; where you direct it determines your trajectory. To achieve meaningful progress, concentrate your efforts on a singular purpose. Avoid dispersing your focus across too many endeavors. By aligning your energy with clear objectives, you enhance your effectiveness and accelerate your path to success.

The Healing Power of Tears

Crying isn't a sign of weakness; it's a natural response that facilitates emotional healing. Emotional tears contain stress hormones and other toxins, and their release can alleviate both physical and emotional pain. This process activates the parasympathetic nervous system, promoting a sense of calm and aiding emotional recovery.

Wisdom Through Experience

Wisdom isn't merely accumulated knowledge; it's the ability to apply insights effectively. As you navigate life's complexities, each experience contributes to a deeper understanding. Embrace learning opportunities and recognize that true wisdom often arises from the willingness to learn from both successes and setbacks.

Decisive Action

Indecision can be paralyzing. When faced with choices, it's essential to act with confidence and clarity. By making informed decisions and committing to them, you create momentum that propels you forward. Trust in your judgment and the process, knowing that each step brings you closer to your goals.

Opportunities in Adversity

Challenges are not roadblocks; they are opportunities in disguise. You can uncover new paths and solutions by reframing obstacles as chances for growth. This mindset shift allows you to harness adversity's potential, transforming difficulties into stepping stones toward success.

Note: Written by Dan McMeans with 20% supported by AI